MISSION SURVIVAL:
SAVING EARTH'S ENDANGERED ANIMALS

SAVING THE
ORANGUTAN

LOUISE SPILSBURY

CHERITON
CHILDREN'S BOOKS

Published in 2023 by **Cheriton Children's Books**
PO Box 7258, Bridgnorth WV16 9ET, UK

© 2023 Cheriton Children's Books

First Edition

Author: Louise Spilsbury
Designer: Paul Myerscough
Editor: Jane Brooke
Proofreader: Tracey Kelly
Consultant: David Hawksett, BSc

Picture credits: Cover: Shutterstock/Lukaszemanphoto. Inside: p1: Shutterstock/Djohan Shahrin; pp4-5: Shutterstock/Milan Zygmunt; pp6-7: Shutterstock/Leolintang; p7bl: Shutterstock/Sergey Uryadnikov; p7br: Shutterstock/Sertan Yaman; p7t: Wikimedia Commons/Tim Laman; p8b: Shutterstock/Akhmad Dody Firmansyah; p9t: Wikimedia Commons/Tim Laman; pp10-11: Shutterstock/Sergey Uryadnikov; pp12-13: Shutterstock/Sergey Uryadnikov; p13b: Shutterstock/Puyalroyo; p13c: Shutterstock/Funny Solution Studio; p13t: Shutterstock/Pat Whelen; pp14-15: Shutterstock/Djohan Shahrin; pp16-17: Shutterstock/Petr Klabal; p17b: Shutterstock/AnnGaysorn; p17t: Shutterstock/AnnGaysorn; pp18-19: Shutterstock/Rich Carey; p19b: Shutterstock/Denys.Kutsevalov; pp20-21: Shutterstock/Erik Zandboer; p20b: Shutterstock/Light And Dark Studio; p21b: Shutterstock/Lightpoet; p21t: Shutterstock/Andrea Izzotti; pp22-23: Shutterstock/Stephane Bidouze; p23b: Shutterstock/Samuel Borges Photography; p23t: Shutterstock/Samuel Borges Photography; pp24-25: Shutterstock/Yogie Hizkia; p25b: Shutterstock/Magic Orb Studio; pp26-27: Shutterstock/Katesalin Pagkaihang; p27b: Shutterstock/David Evison; p27c: Shutterstock/Sertan Yaman; p27t: Shutterstock/Sergey Uryadnikov; pp28-29: Shutterstock/Muan Sibero; p28b: Shutterstock/Anton Balazh; p29b: Shutterstock/Ground Picture; p29t: Shutterstock/Ground Picture; pp30-31: Shutterstock/Donny Sophandi; p31b: Shutterstock/Katoosha; pp32-33: Shutterstock/Don Mammoser; p33b: Shutterstock/Torsten Pursche; p33c: Shutterstock/Katesalin Pagkaihang; p33t: Shutterstock/Wise Dog Studio; pp34-35: Shutterstock/Various photo; p35b: Shutterstock/Krakenimages.com; p35t: Shutterstock/Krakenimages.com; pp36-37: Shutterstock/Boule; p37b: Shutterstock/Adi Haririe; p38b: Shutterstock/Gudkov Andrey; p39b: Shutterstock/Daniel Io Eyre; p39t: Shutterstock/Valerijs Novickis; pp40-41: Shutterstock/Captain Al; p41b: Shutterstock/Oleg Golovnev; p41t: Shutterstock/Oleg Golovnev; p42: Shutterstock/Sergey Panikratov; p43: Shutterstock/Urbanbuzz; p44: Shutterstock/Lena Viridis; p45: Shutterstock/Mentatdgt.

Printed in China

Publisher's Note: The information in the Kids on a Mission features in this book are suggestions for actions that children can take to help protect endangered animals, based on extensive research by the author and consultant. The email addresses and the children featured in the photographs are for illustrative purposes only.

Please visit our website,
www.cheritonchildrensbooks.com,
to see more of our high-quality books.

CONTENTS

INTRODUCTION
ORANGUTANS IN DANGER _ _ _ _ _ _ _ _ _ _ _ _ _ 4

CHAPTER ONE
MEET THE ORANGUTAN _ _ _ _ _ _ _ _ _ _ _ _ _ 6

CHAPTER TWO
HOMES UNDER THREAT _ _ _ _ _ _ _ _ _ _ _ _ _ 16

CHAPTER THREE
UNDER THREAT FROM HUNTING _ _ _ _ _ _ _ _ _ 22

CHAPTER FOUR
CLIMATE CHANGE _ _ _ _ _ _ _ _ _ _ _ _ _ _ _ _ 28

CHAPTER FIVE
OTHER THREATS TO ORANGUTANS _ _ _ _ _ _ _ 34

CONCLUSION
WHAT'S NEXT FOR THE ORANGUTAN? _ _ _ _ _ _ 40

MAKE IT YOUR MISSION:
A CAREER IN CONSERVATION _ _ _ _ _ _ _ _ _ _ _ 42
CAREERS IN CONSERVATION _ _ _ _ _ _ _ _ _ _ _ 44

GLOSSARY _ _ _ _ _ _ _ _ _ _ _ _ _ _ _ _ _ _ _ 46
FIND OUT MORE _ _ _ _ _ _ _ _ _ _ _ _ _ _ _ _ 47
INDEX AND ABOUT THE AUTHOR _ _ _ _ _ _ _ _ 48

ORANGUTANS IN DANGER

The name *orangutan* comes from Malaysian and Indonesian words. It means "person of the forest." Orangutans are so-named because they look very similar to humans. However, there are some big differences between humans and orangutans. Orangutans are covered in shaggy orange hair and have very long arms. They also live in trees. These incredible animals are very special. They are the only **great apes** in Asia.

FACING THREATS FROM HUMANS

One hundred years ago, more than 230,000 orangutans lived on Earth. Today, only around 70,000 orangutans can still be found in the wild. That is because their homes have been destroyed by human activities. People are cutting down the forests in which orangutans live to make room for homes, **mines**, and farms. Orangutans have also been hunted in huge numbers by humans. They are killed for food or because people believe the animals are pests.

Orangutans face an increasing ▶ risk of extinction. That means that they could die out, leaving no orangutans on Earth.

NOT TOO LATE TO SAVE

There is a real danger that if we do not do more to help orangutans, one day they may be gone forever. **Conservationists** are doing all they can to save the remaining orangutans on Earth, and they need our help. It is very important to protect these incredible animals before it is too late to save them.

"... orangutans have been living for hundreds of thousands of years in their forest—living fantastic lives, never **overpopulating**, never destroying the forest."

Jane Goodall, great apes expert

HELP THE ORANGUTAN!

There is still hope for the orangutan, and it is not too late to save it. People everywhere have heard the orangutan's call for help. And they are making it their mission to help these amazing animals survive. In this book, we'll learn about the orangutan and why it is in danger. We'll discover what people are doing to help orangutans and how they have built a career in **conservation**. We'll find out how kids everywhere can make it their mission to help save the orangutan. And we'll learn how you could make a career in conservation your mission. Feeling mission-ready? Then read on!

The International Union for Conservation of Nature (IUCN) keeps a record of the world's **species** and how at risk of extinction they are. It is called the

Red List.

There are more than

142,500

species on the Red List.

All orangutans are now considered

endangered.

CHAPTER ONE

MEET THE ORANGUTAN

Orangutans are the largest animals that live almost entirely in trees. Orangutans have special features that help them survive in the forest.

SUPERLONG ARMS

From fingertip to fingertip, orangutans have an arm span of more than 7 feet (2.2 m). Their arms are one-and-a-half times longer than their legs! As well as long arms, orangutans also have flexible knees and ankle joints. They use them to jump, twist, grip, and balance as they swing from branch to branch.

FINGERS TO TOES

All orangutans have unique fingerprints and toe prints, just like humans. They also have fingernails and toenails rather than claws. Orangutans use their nails to clean and scratch themselves. They also use their nails to prize open the fruits and nuts they eat.

BIG AND SMALL

When standing, male orangutans are about 5 feet (1.5 m) tall. Females are shorter. They are about 4 feet (1.2 m) tall. Adult male orangutans can weigh up to 200 pounds (90 kg). Females are lighter. They weigh up to 110 pounds (50 kg).

PUFFED UP

Some adult male orangutans have large cheek pads on the sides of their face. They are called flanges. The flanges make the adult males look more impressive. The flanges also help make an orangutan's calls louder, so they can be heard through the forest.

MAKING A NOISE

Orangutans have a sac that hangs from their throats. It is a little like a pouch. Throat sacs can be very big on older males. They can be inflated, or blown up, to make the animals' calls reach long distances. Some orangutan calls have been heard up to 1 mile (1.6 km) away!

Tapanuli orangutan

Bornean orangutan

In a Group

Scientists group animals to help them classify, or order, them. Orangutans belong to a group of animals called *Pongo*. There are three types of orangutan in this group. They are the Sumatran orangutan (*Pongo abelii*), the Bornean orangutan (*Pongo pygmaeus*), and the Tapanuli orangutan (*Pongo tapanuliensis*).

Sumatran orangutan

WHERE ORANGUTANS LIVE

In the past, orangutans were found throughout large areas of Asia. They lived as far north as southern China and as far south as the Indonesian island of Java. Today, orangutans are found only in two places on Earth. They are the Indonesian islands of Borneo and Sumatra, in Southeast Asia.

RAIN FOREST LIFE

Orangutans live mainly among the tall trees of **tropical rain forests**. The warm, wet weather in tropical areas allows rain forest trees to grow very tall. Most orangutans live in forests that are remote, or far from people. The animals also prefer to live near waterways and not too high up mountains. Orangutans tend to live alone, but they have large home ranges that may overlap with other orangutans. A home range is the area of land in which an animal lives and moves about. An adult female lives in a home range of about 3.5 square miles (9 sq km). An adult male's **territory** can be as large as 15 square miles (39 sq km).

HABITAT UNDER THREAT

The Tapanuli orangutan is the most endangered species of great ape. The Tapanuli orangutan was described as a **distinct species** as recently as 2017. Unfortunately, there are plans to build a **hydroelectric dam** through this precious animal's **habitat**. Building the dam would mean clearing large areas of forest and flooding the Tapanuli orangutan's main habitat with water. That would put these amazing animals at a far greater risk of extinction.

◀ The building of hydroelectric dams such as this one in orangutan habitat puts the endangered animals at even greater risk.

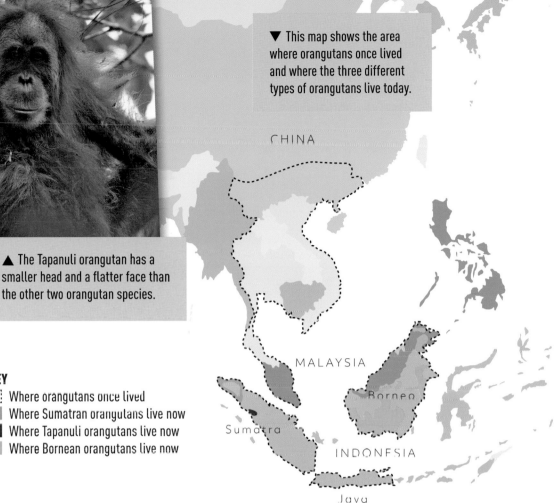

▼ This map shows the area where orangutans once lived and where the three different types of orangutans live today.

CHINA

▲ The Tapanuli orangutan has a smaller head and a flatter face than the other two orangutan species.

KEY
- Where orangutans once lived
- Where Sumatran orangutans live now
- Where Tapanuli orangutans live now
- Where Bornean orangutans live now

MALAYSIA

Borneo

Sumatra

INDONESIA

Java

STILL LIVING IN THE WILD

The number of orangutans still living in the wild varies between species. The Bornean orangutan lives in rain forests, swamps, and mountain forests on the island of Borneo. Borneo is the third-largest island in the world. Despite that, around only 55,000 Bornean orangutans remain in the wild. The Sumatran orangutan is only found in the north of the island of Sumatra. There are around just 14,000 Sumatran orangutans in the wild. The Tapanuli orangutan lives in one small area of rain forest only, the Tapanuli district of north Sumatra. There are fewer than 800 Tapanuli orangutans living in the wild.

WHY SHOULD WE HELP THE ORANGUTAN?

We should help orangutans because they help us! Orangutans play a very important role in their **environment**—they help keep their forest home healthy. That helps all the plants and animals that live in the forest, and it helps humans, too.

Orangutans are a keystone ▶ species. That means that all the other **organisms** in their ecosystem depend on them.

FOREST GARDENERS

Orangutans are known as gardeners of the forest. That is because they help spread seeds around. Orangutans eat a lot of fruit from the trees. The seeds pass through the animals' gut in one piece. The complete seeds come out in orangutan dung, or waste, hours later. As orangutans move around, the seeds are dropped far from the trees on which they grew. That gives the seeds a better chance of growing into healthy new trees. An added bonus is that the orangutan dung acts like **fertilizer** and helps the plants grow.

THE FOREST NEEDS ORANGUTANS

If we protect orangutans, we also protect all the other plants and animals that live in their habitat. If these places are kept healthy for orangutans, they are kept healthy for every other organism, or living thing, that exists there, too. Without orangutans spreading seeds, the forests in which orangutans live would look very different. That would affect all the people and animals that live in or use those forests. The people of Borneo and Sumatra depend on the orangutans' forest for food and water. Many earn money from working in the forest, too.

What Is an Ecosystem?

An ecosystem is a group of natural parts that all work together for a purpose. Ecosystems include nonliving things such as water, sunshine, and air. These are called abiotic factors. Ecosystems also include living things such as plants and animals. These are called biotic factors. The living things in an ecosystem depend on the abiotic factors in the ecosystem to survive. Every part of the ecosystem has an important part to play. A healthy ecosystem has many different plants and animals living together. If any part of that ecosystem changes or is damaged, the other parts are affected, too.

ORANGUTAN MEALTIMES

Orangutans love fruit! In fact, they eat more than 300 different types of fruit. Orangutans forage, or search for food, during the day. They spend up to six hours a day foraging or eating.

FRUIT FEEDERS

Orangutans eat almost any fruit they can find. When fruit is scarce, orangutans eat young leaves and shoots, insects, soil, tree bark, and vines. They also sometimes eat eggs and small animals such as birds and fish. They get the water they need from the fruit that they eat, but they may also drink from puddles of water that collect in tree holes.

SMELLY SUPPERS

One of the orangutan's favorite fruits is a huge spiky fruit called durian. The fruit has a horrible smell, but that doesn't stop the orangutan from eating it! The orangutan uses its teeth and hands to break open the hard shell of the fruit.

FEEDING WITH THEIR FEET

Orangutans use both their hands and feet to collect food as they travel through the trees. Orangutans can grip, peel, and break off pieces of food using their hands or feet.

TOOL USE

Some Sumatran orangutans use tools to get their food. They use sticks to pick out **termites**, ants, or bees from tree holes. The smart animals also wrap leaves around their hands to handle prickly fruits or thorny branches.

MIGHTY MOUTHS

Orangutans have very strong jaws. They can crack, crush, and chew tough foods. The foods include the spiny coverings of some fruit, nuts, and tree bark. Orangutans use their lips to test the **texture** of food before biting into it.

PEOPLE ON A MISSION

There is no doubt that the orangutan is under threat. This amazing species is in a struggle for survival. However, it is not on its own in the battle. Many people around the world have made it their mission to help precious orangutans survive.

PEOPLE ON THE GROUND

People working on the ground include wildlife managers, rangers, and officers. These conservation workers help protect the orangutan's home and monitor its numbers. They collect data, or information, on orangutans and the health of their habitat. Public educators and outreach specialists work with local people to educate them about orangutans.

PEOPLE IN OFFICES

Many people who work for conservation organizations work in offices. Some work with governments and companies based in countries where orangutans live. They develop ways to protect the orangutans and their habitats. **Communications** and public relations experts work for charities and conservation organizations. They alert people everywhere about the threat to orangutans. People who work in charities raise money to pay for projects to save orangutans.

PEOPLE IN LABORATORIES

Some scientists who help orangutans work in zoos or labs. Zoologists and wildlife technicians are scientists who study animals such as orangutans to find out more about them. For example, scientists in a lab have discovered that orangutans need to eat a huge amount of fruit to build the strong muscles required to swing through trees. They also study data that other conservationists collect.

PEOPLE EVERYWHERE

One thing that we all can do is to learn as much as we can about orangutans and the challenges they face. Then, we can tell other people what we have learned. We can also join organizations that help orangutans. We can raise money to save orangutans and encourage our friends and family to help us.

MAKE IT YOUR MISSION

You could help orangutans and other endangered animals by taking action and planning a career in conservation. Here's how:

1. In this book, you'll discover what actions kids on a mission can take to help orangutans. Use them to inspire your own actions to rescue orangutans.
2. You'll also discover some of the careers people on a mission have in orangutan conservation. As you read about each one, think about whether that career in conservation might suit you.
3. At the end of this book, you'll find a guide to how to build a career in conservation. Check it out to discover how you can make saving animals your life mission.

▲ If baby orangutan orphans are found in the forest by wildlife rangers, they may be taken to a special center where they can be cared for.

CHAPTER TWO

HOMES UNDER THREAT

Between 1900 and 2000, the **population** of Indonesia grew from roughly 15 million to more than 200 million. And the number of people in the country keeps on growing. All those people need space in which to live and find the **resources** they need to survive. That is bad news for orangutans.

LOSING RAIN FORESTS

Deforestation is the cutting down of forests on a large scale. It is the number one threat to orangutans. As the human population grows, forests are being cut down to make way for homes and farmland. Towns and villages are built on orangutan land. New roads are built that cut through the land. That makes it more difficult for orangutans to travel long distances to find the food they need. It also makes it more difficult for them to find a **mate**, so they can **breed**.

TAKING OVER LAND

Orangutan land is also being taken over by people in industry. Loggers are people who cut down the trees in forests using chain saws and bulldozers. They use the wood for **timber**. Trees are also cut down to make paper products, such as toilet paper. Those products are sold to people all over the world. People also clear the land on which orangutans live to dig mines and grow **plantations** of palm oil. In the early 1970s, more than three-quarters of Borneo was covered in forests. Between 1973 and 2015, more than half of that area of forest was destroyed.

"If the current destruction of the rain forest continues, then I have absolutely no hope that any orangutans will remain in the wild."

Alan Knight, from International Animal Rescue (IAR)

SAFETY IN THE RAIN FOREST

To help protect orangutans, conservationists have set up conservation areas where they can safely live. The areas include national parks or wildlife **reserves**. They are parts of the rain forest in which orangutan habitats are kept safe from logging, farming, and mining. Wildlife reserves are monitored by people working in wildlife conservation, who try and keep orangutans and other animals safe.

▲ Orangutans are built for a life in the forest, and without trees they cannot survive.

Kids on a Mission

 @joe4orang-2006

When I found out that orangutan homes are being destroyed to make toilet paper, I told my mom. Now we buy only recycled toilet paper.

SPOTLIGHT ON

PALM OIL PLANTATIONS

One of the biggest threats to orangutans is the spread of palm oil plantations in Borneo and Sumatra. Palm oil is the most widely used vegetable oil in the world. It is a very useful product. It is found in many of the products we buy, from cookies to toothpaste. The problem with palm oil lies in the method used to grow palm oil trees. Palm oil trees grow best in flat, wet tropical areas—exactly where rain forests grow. Huge areas of tropical rain forest are being cleared to make room for palm oil plantations.

HOMELESS ORANGUTANS

People often burn down rain forests when they clear land for palm oil plantations. Fire is a useful way of getting rid of trees quickly. The other advantage of burning forests is that plantation farmers do not need to add a lot of chemical fertilizer to the land to help the palm trees grow. When forest land is cleared by fire, the ash from the burned trees acts as a fertilizer for the soil. However, some orangutans are killed in the land-clearing fires. Others die of starvation when their food supply is burned down. Orangutans are also killed by farmers if they return to plantation areas to try and get food.

▼ Palm oil is a huge industry. Palm oil is Indonesia's most valuable farm export, or product that is sold overseas.

palm oil plantation

PEOPLE ON A MISSION: ORANGUTAN HELPERS

Wildlife **policy** analysts and wildlife consultants work with governments and industries. They encourage good environmental practices, such as persuading companies to grow **sustainable** palm oil. Sustainable palm oil comes from palm oil trees that were planted on already damaged land rather than healthy rain forest. Another benefit of palm oil trees is that they produce far more oil than other oil-producing crops, such as sunflower oil. For that reason, much less land is required to grow palm oil trees than plants that produce other types of oil.

Public educators and outreach specialists encourage the public to buy only sustainable palm oil products. They teach people about orangutans and their habitats. They work with local people and educate them about orangutans and the importance of protecting them.

Wildlife managers monitor orangutan populations and their forest habitats. They create management plans for orangutan areas. For example, they educate people about the need for reserves and wildlife corridors. They are stretches of land between reserves or areas where orangutans live that are protected from being cleared for plantations or other developments. That allows orangutans to move freely between different areas.

◀ Orangutans are even at risk of being captured or shot when they try to escape forest that is being cleared for farmland.

SHARING A HABITAT

Many other animals live alongside the orangutan in its wild habitat. Many of these creatures are also under threat from human activities such as hunting and forest clearing.

THE SUMATRAN RHINO

Today, there are fewer than 80 Sumatran rhinos left in the wild. In the past, **poaching** reduced their numbers. Their biggest threat is now habitat loss. As forests are destroyed, more rhinos are lost. Conservationists are trying to breed Sumatran rhinos in **captivity**. The hope is that the baby rhinos can then be released into the wild to boost the rhino population.

THE SUMATRAN TIGER

Sumatran tigers have thicker black stripes than other tigers. There are fewer than 400 of these animals left in the wild. They live in patches of forest on the island of Sumatra. These forests are under threat from deforestation and poaching. As a result, there is a real danger that the Sumatran tiger could become extinct.

THE LARGE FLYING FOX

The large flying fox is not a fox at all. It is a bat! Large flying foxes live in tropical forests. They use their sharp claws to hang from the branches of large trees. The large flying fox is under threat from habitat destruction. It is also sometimes hunted for food. In some areas, farmers kill the bats to keep them from feeding on their orchards.

THE MALAYAN TAPIR

The Malayan tapir is found throughout the tropical lowland rain forests of Southeast Asia, including Sumatra in Indonesia. It is under threat from habitat destruction, because much of the forest in which it lives has been cleared for farming. Its habitat has also been flooded for hydroelectric dams.

21

CHAPTER THREE

UNDER THREAT FROM HUNTING

People have hunted orangutans for thousands of years. Remains of orangutans have been found in **prehistoric** sites in China, Vietnam, and Thailand. These finds show that orangutans were easy **prey** for hungry prehistoric hunters. As humans developed better weapons, they killed more and more orangutans. Their hunting of orangutans caused their numbers to drop drastically. Today, orangutans still face the threat of being hunted.

STILL IN DANGER

Today, it is against the law to kill orangutans. Yet, the animals are still being killed. Fewer local people now kill orangutans for food, but some people are so poor, they feel they have no choice but to do so. They also poach orangutans and sell the animals' meat or body parts for money. Meat from orangutans is called bushmeat. Bushmeat is meat that comes from a wild animal. The animals' body parts are made into medicine.

Orangutans are an ▶ easy target for hunters. That is because they are large, which makes them easy to spot. They also often sit still for long periods of time. When they do move, they move slowly, which also makes them easy to kill.

DEALING IN DEATH

When logging companies or palm oil plantation workers cut down trees at the edges of forests or to make roads, it is easier for poachers to reach orangutans. Poachers also use these roads to transport dead orangutans from the forest. Skulls and other body parts are sold to people, who keep them to show off to others. When adult females are killed, poachers sell the babies, too.

Kids on a Mission

@orangprotect-127

I have created a blog to tell people about the dangers that orangutans face. A lot of people have contacted me to tell me they didn't realize orangutans were so endangered.

"The simple conclusion is that orangutans will be hunted to extinction unless someone stops the killings."

Erik Meijaard, author of a study into orangutan poaching

SPOTLIGHT ON

PLANTATION KILLINGS

Some orangutans are killed by people who believe that the animals are pests. That usually happens when hungry orangutans stray into farmland, villages, or plantations when looking for food. When orangutans ruin crops, a farmer and their family may starve. Angry farmers may then shoot, beat, and hack the orangutans. One orangutan was found riddled with 130 pellets. It had also been attacked with a large knife.

Palm oil is big business ▶ in Indonesia, and many people depend on it for a living. Around 4 million people in the country work in the industry.

COMPANY KILLERS

When orangutans search for food in a plantation, they eat young palm seedlings. They also tend to destroy young palm plants. For that reason, palm oil companies pay local people to find and kill any orangutans found within plantations. Hunters often chop off an orangutan's hand, to prove to the company that they killed the animal. They are then paid for the kill. If hunters find an adult female orangutan with a baby, they usually kill the mother and take the baby to sell it as a pet. Palm oil plantation workers are sometimes paid to kill orangutans even before they clear the forest where the animals live.

PEOPLE ON A MISSION: PROTECTING ORANGUTANS

Wildlife rangers and officers work hard to protect orangutans. One of their jobs is to patrol forest areas. They often decide where to patrol based on information about where hunters have been seen. Hunting camps are usually dotted around the forest. When rangers find a hunting camp, they destroy it. If they find people who have killed an orangutan, they arrest them.

Wildlife protection officers work to ensure that palm oil and logging companies do not take over more orangutan habitat. They watch for any attempts by such companies to illegally cut down more trees. They also rescue any orangutans that have entered plantations or have been injured by hunters. They take them to vets, so they can be treated. They then release the animals back into areas of protected rain forest.

Some officers work with local people. They help them find ways of earning money that do not harm orangutans. Some former hunters now work as wildlife rangers and patrol forests to keep orangutans safe. Some rescue injured orangutans and return them to a safe part of the forest when they are well again. Working in conservation gives local people paid work and encourages them to protect orangutans.

▲ Rescued orangutans like this baby are given health checks and are cared for until well.

25

ORANGUTAN BABIES

When a female orangutan is killed by hunters, it has a terrible impact on her baby. Just like human babies, baby orangutans rely on their moms for a very long time.

NEST FOR A NEWBORN

A female orangutan usually gives birth in a nest high up in the trees. She makes the nest from folded branches. She weaves the branches together carefully, so her newborn baby does not fall through a gap in the nest.

CUTE BABIES

Orangutans usually give birth to one baby at a time. They sometimes have twins. Newly born orangutans have pink faces. The faces change to dark brown or black as the babies grow older. The babies have cute tufts of hair on their head that stand upright!

HOLD TIGHT!

For the first few weeks of its life, an orangutan baby holds tight to its mother's belly as she swings through the trees looking for fruit. When the baby grows a little older, it gets better at balancing. Then, it rides on its mother's back, so it can see all around.

NURSING MOTHERS

By the time an orangutan is four or five years old, it moves around on its own. However, it never goes far from its mom. That's because the young animal is still nursing. Nursing means that a mother feeds her baby with milk from her body. Young orangutans may nurse for up to seven years, so they stay near their mom all that time.

NURSERY SCHOOL

Young orangutans learn everything from their moms. They discover where to find fruit, what is good to eat, and where to sleep in the trees at night. When they have learned all these skills, they stop nursing. They then leave their moms and start to live on their own.

27

CHAPTER FOUR

CLIMATE CHANGE

Climate change is causing problems all over our planet. It is making Earth's **atmosphere** heat up, which is causing more extreme patterns of weather all over the world. That is having a hugely negative impact on habitats, humans, and wildlife such as orangutans.

WHAT IS CLIMATE CHANGE?

Climate change describes the average weather conditions in a region over a long period of time. Earth's climate has changed slowly for the entire history of our planet. The changes were due to natural causes such as changes in the sun and **geological** activity. The difference with the climate change that is happening now is that it is caused by human activities. They include burning **fossil fuels**, which releases gases into Earth's atmosphere. The gases surround the planet like a blanket, causing the Earth to heat up. Changes in temperature in Earth's atmosphere affect the planet's weather patterns in different ways.

Climate change poses ▶ a real threat to the survival of orangutans and their habitats.

Burning fossil fuels to ▶ make the electricity that powers our lights and machines releases gases that cause climate change.

FOREST EFFECTS

Climate change is affecting the orangutan's forest home in two devastating ways. First, it is causing an increase in the amount of rainfall. That interferes with plant **reproduction** because it damages the flowers and keeps them from producing the fruits in which seeds develop. That reduces the amount of fruit available to orangutans. There is **evidence** that orangutans are less likely to reproduce when food is scarce. Females are less likely to become pregnant when they don't get enough fruit to eat. Second, climate change causes more forest fires. That reduces orangutan habitat and further reduces fruit trees from which orangutans can feed.

"Never before have we had such an awareness of what we are doing to the planet, and never before have we had the power to do something about that."

Sir David Attenborough, broadcaster and writer

Kids on a Mission

@carrie4Earth-56

I do what I can to help stop climate change. For example, I turn off lights when I leave a room, and I turn off my computer when I'm not using it.

SPOTLIGHT ON FOREST FIRES

Indonesia has two seasons in a year. It rains heavily during the wet season, and it is mostly very hot with little rain in the dry season. However, climate change is making wet seasons wetter, but it is also making dry seasons drier and longer. When that happens, the land becomes **parched**. A long period with little or no rain is called a drought. During a drought, trees and other plants become very dry. As a result, forest fires can spread quickly and rage out of control.

FIRE DAMAGE

Some orangutans burn to death in the flames if they cannot outrun the forest fires. For example, between 1997 and 1998, forest fires in Kalimantan killed 8,000 orangutans. Even once a fire has stopped, it continues to threaten orangutans. After a forest fire, the animals may starve. They cannot find enough food because their fruit trees have been burned down. Fire also breaks up areas of forest. That makes it more difficult for orangutans to reach areas where they might find food or a mate.

PEOPLE ON A MISSION: FIGHTING CLIMATE CHANGE

Some climate and environmental scientists conduct research on climate change. They study the effects of climate change on habitats and animals. Some of these scientists focus on the effects of climate change on forests and orangutans. For example, they research which types of trees to grow when replanting forest areas. They choose trees that will be better able to survive drought and that will be able to produce fruit that orangutans can eat.

Some climate and environmental scientists research how rain forests can help to prevent climate change. They gather evidence such as the amount of **carbon dioxide (CO2)** an area of orangutan rain forest can absorb every year. Other conservationists can use this information to persuade more governments to get involved with rain forest protection. That will give the world more time to reduce our dependence on fossil fuels.

Environment lawyers may be employed by organizations and governments that try and help protect orangutans. Some lawyers act against businesses or individuals that break laws that are intended to protect orangutans. For example, some people are taken to court for starting fires that can rage out of control in forests during droughts.

▲ Breathing in smoke from forest fires can affect the health of orangutans.

ORANGUTANS NEED TREES

Orangutans spend 95 percent of their lives in the trees. Trees provide orangutans with food, shelter, and safety from dangerous predators. Predators are animals that hunt and eat other animals.

SAFETY IN THE TREES

Orangutans in Sumatra rarely come down to the ground. They stay in the trees. There, they are out of reach of many dangerous predators such as tigers, clouded leopards, large pythons, and crocodiles. Those predators don't live in Borneo, so orangutans on that island come down to the ground more often.

FRUIT MAPS

The different fruit trees in a rain forest flower and produce fruit at different times. Young orangutans learn to keep a map of their forest area in their mind. That helps them find ripe fruit all year around. When forests burn down and orangutans are forced to move to a new area, they no longer have this important mental food map. It is then much more difficult for them to find food.

BORN TO LIVE IN TREES

Orangutans swing gracefully through the trees. However, orangutans are very slow and awkward when walking on the ground.

NESTS FOR THE NIGHT

Orangutans make a new nest in which to sleep every night by folding branches together. They use smaller branches to make a mattress. They weave together flexible branches to make the nest tight and secure.

OTHER THREATS TO ORANGUTANS

Orangutans face other threats, too. Many baby orangutans are stolen from their families and forest homes to become pets. Many orangutan pets develop very serious health problems.

ORANGUTANS FOR SALE

Since 1931, keeping an orangutan as a pet has been illegal under Indonesian and international law. Despite that, it is believed that between 200 and 500 baby orangutans are sold on the international illegal wildlife market every year. That number could be even higher. Some orangutans are kept as pets. Others are kept as a status symbol, or something that people believe shows how wealthy they are. Orangutans are also often poached from the wild for the entertainment industry. For example, orangutans have been used illegally in kickboxing tournaments in Thailand.

"Keeping orangutans as pets could make them lose their instincts for living in the wild."

Ruswanto, an official from the IAR

▼ Captured orangutans may be made to perform in shows, such as this one, to entertain people. That is cruel and puts the species in danger.

A DEADLY BUSINESS

The only way for an orangutan baby to be caught is for the mother to be killed. Then, the hunters rip the baby from its mother's dead body. Many babies die during journeys in which they are **smuggled** from Borneo and Sumatra to overseas places. People who buy orangutans may try and care for the animals, but orangutans are not suitable pets. People may not provide them with the right foods. The babies can then become sick.

Kids on a Mission

@hope4apes-2005

I've been learning more about what the illegal wildlife trade is and how I can help stop it. I share all the information I can online to encourage others to help stop the trade, too.

AGAINST THE LAW

The illegal **trade** of orangutans is a major threat to the animals' survival. It is made worse by habitat destruction. When rain forest trees are cut down, orangutans have nowhere to go and spend more time on the ground. This increases the chances of them being found and caught by loggers or plantation workers.

SPOTLIGHT ON CAPTIVITY

Many of the orangutans kept in captivity are badly treated. Those kept in zoos are much better cared for. In zoos, scientists can study the orangutans, too. Some zoos are also involved in conservation breeding programs. That means that they are allowed to breed orangutans to prevent the species from becoming extinct. Although these animals can't yet be released into the wild safely, it is hoped that one day they might be.

ORANGUTANS IN ZOOS

Many of the orangutans we see in zoos today were born in captivity. They could not be safely released into the wild because they would not survive. In good zoos, they are safe and cared for. Zookeepers make sure that the orangutans have day-to-day activities that keep them active and occupied. That keeps the animals from becoming bored and inactive. Education is also an essential part of conservation. When people visit zoos and learn about the animals there, they are more likely to care about protecting them and their habitats.

PEOPLE ON A MISSION: ORANGUTAN SCIENTISTS

Some scientists specialize in helping orangutans. Zoologists in zoos study them, so that they understand how the animals normally behave. Zoologists also study the way orangutans think, for example, by playing fun memory games with them. That can help them understand what orangutans need in the wild.

Orangutans rescued from the illegal wildlife trade spend years in a rehabilitation center. That is a place where animals are helped to recover from injuries or poor treatment. Scientists there teach orangutans to climb trees, find fruit, and build sleeping nests. When orangutans are ready to start spending long periods of time alone in the forest, technicians track the animals to make sure they're eating well and dealing with the wild. Every orangutan released into the wild is **tagged** so it can be easily monitored.

Some scientists work with **Geographic Information Systems (GIS)** and other technologies to collect and study data to help wildlife and its habitats. In Borneo, scientists use GIS to map and analyze orangutan habitats and identify areas that need protection. They also use GIS to locate and track fires, so that they can alert local forestry departments to put out fires early.

▲ It is much better for orangutans to live in the wild, but those in good-quality zoos are safe from poaching, climate change, and habitat loss.

Many of the people who work with ▶ captive orangutans in places such as zoos and conservation centers truly care for these amazing animals.

OTHER GREAT APES IN DANGER

Around the world, other great apes are in danger. Many of them face similar challenges to the orangutan. They are rapidly losing much of their forest habitat to human activities such as farming, mining, and logging.

THE BONOBO

Bonobos are roughly the same size as chimpanzees. They have longer legs and tend to walk upright more often than chimpanzees, which often walk on all fours. Bonobos live in tropical forests in the Democratic Republic of Congo (DRC). There are wars and fighting between different groups in that country. There is also poverty in the area. Both factors have increased the risks to bonobos of poaching and habitat destruction.

THE GORILLA

Gorillas are the largest and strongest apes in the world. They live in remote forests in Africa. Their numbers are decreasing for several reasons. Like orangutans, gorillas keep forests healthy by spreading seeds that grow into new trees. Large numbers of gorillas have been hunted and killed by humans. They are killed for their meat. They are also killed so that their body parts or their babies can be sold. People have taken over gorilla land to make space for farms and mines.

THE CHIMPANZEE

The chimpanzee suffers similar threats to the orangutan. They include habitat loss, poaching, and disease. Chimpanzees share up to 98 percent of the same **deoxyribonucleic acid (DNA)** as humans. Biologically, they are more closely related to humans than they are to gorillas. For that reason, another risk facing these great apes is being infected with human diseases. Chimpanzees eat a variety of plant foods, and they sometimes hunt and eat small **mammals** such as monkeys. Chimpanzees can use tools. For example, they use sticks to fish out insects from trees. They also crack open nuts with rocks. If they survive human threats, chimpanzees can live for around 50 years in the wild.

WHAT'S NEXT FOR THE ORANGUTAN?

It is difficult to say what the future holds for orangutans. These peaceful and intelligent animals face many threats, and orangutan populations are fragile. A female orangutan has just three or four babies in her lifetime. That means that the loss of just one orangutan has a big effect on a population. The good news is that many people are working to save orangutans. They are on a mission to ensure the animals' survival.

HELP FROM CONSERVATIONISTS

Conservationists are encouraging countries to sign up to international agreements that protect orangutan habitats. At a climate change conference in 2021, world leaders agreed to end deforestation by 2030. Conservationists need to push to make sure that this happens. In the meantime, they are working on projects to replant forests and build bridges for orangutans to move around forests safely. They also work with TRAFFIC, the wildlife trade monitoring network. They hope to stop the illegal trade in orangutans as pets. In the future, the world will need more conservationists to help protect wildlife from the threats it faces.

> "We are making hard-won progress, but there is a long way to go with forests being lost or damaged rapidly across the world."

Will Ashley-Cantello, chief adviser on forests for World Wildlife Fund (WWF) UK

HELP FROM ORGANIZATIONS

Conservation organizations such as the WWF work hard to save orangutans and other wildlife. They put pressure on governments to improve their laws to ensure that orangutans and their habitats are protected. They work to increase the number of orangutan reserves, so that more orangutans can live in safety. They campaign to ensure that, in the future, all palm oil is produced without deforestation.

HELP FROM ALL OF US

We can all make a difference. Even small actions can help. We can encourage our families to buy sustainable products that do not contribute to deforestation. We can help prevent further climate change by bicycling to school or car sharing. We can learn more about the dangers to orangutans and tell everyone we know about the threats. Orangutans are in danger, but there is hope. If we all work together, we can save these incredible animals.

Kids on a Mission

 @ecoaction_jenna

When I grow up, I'm going to get a job in conservation. I want to do all I can to save wild orangutans and their amazing rain forest homes.

MAKE IT YOUR MISSION: A CAREER IN CONSERVATION

If you care about the future of orangutans and other endangered animals, why not make protecting them your mission? You can do this by planning for a future career in conservation. On pages 44–45, you'll find some of the conservation careers that are possible. And here are things you can do right now to prepare for a career in conservation and help save orangutans.

STUDY WELL
Conservation careers are popular, so competition for them is fierce. Get ahead by working hard at school now. Concentrate in your science, English, and geography classes. Language classes could also prove useful. If you get a job overseas, being able to speak a foreign language will be very helpful.

GET EXPERIENCE
Work experience is valuable whatever career you choose. Getting work experience in wildlife conservation will help you find the best fit for you in a future career. Work experience gives you the skills you need, too. Try volunteering at a local zoo or wildlife park, wildlife charity, or conservation organization as soon as you are old enough.

▼ There are a lot of ways to get involved in conservation. For example, you could help set up and run a WWF stand at a local festival.

GET INVOLVED

Join a conservation group or wildlife charity today. That is a great way to get in touch with other people who care about wildlife and to learn more about what you can do to help endangered animals. By getting involved with charities and conservation organizations now, you will also prove to future employers that you have always been interested in conservation.

TAKE ACTION!

You have learned about some of the actions that help orangutans from the Kids on a Mission features in this book. Here are some more ideas for other activities that can help protect orangutans:

- Adopt an orangutan! Ask your parents to help you check out the WWF site for information about adopting orangutans.
- Ask your school to hold a fundraising event to raise money for an organization such as WWF and help them protect orangutans.
- Ask your parents to buy furniture and wooden items that come from forests that are sustainably managed.
- Choose recycled tissue and toilet paper. These products are not made from paper from trees that are cut down in rain forests.
- Start a blog about orangutans and the dangers they face. Educate as many people as you can.

FSC

Thank you trees

By choosing products with ▶ FSC labels, you are helping to take care of the world's forests.

CAREERS IN CONSERVATION

There are many different types of conservation careers. The one you choose will depend on your specific areas of interest and your particular talents and skills. Here is information about some of them. You can find out about other conservation jobs on page 47 of this book.

▲ Wildlife managers record data from camera traps as they observe endangered wild animals in a reserve.

WILDLIFE MANAGER

Wildlife managers work on the ground in wild habitats. They have a variety of different duties. If you became one, you would spend time monitoring the animal populations in your area. You could do that in different ways. You might count animals by estimating populations from dung **samples**. You might also check evidence of wildlife on a camera trap. In the case of orangutans, you would probably estimate populations from the number of nests observed. You would also keep a watchful eye on any changes to the habitat and keep a lookout for poachers.

WILDLIFE FORENSICS SPECIALIST

A wildlife **forensics** specialist is a scientist who uses special techniques to investigate wildlife crimes. If you took on this role you would analyze animals, animal parts and products, and other evidence collected by wildlife inspectors and other officials. You would also identify the species to which an animal, part, or product belongs. You might also have to figure out how the animal was killed, by studying evidence from items, suspects, and crime scenes.

PUBLIC RELATIONS OFFICER

If your skills include talking to people and writing, you could consider working as a public relations officer. In that role, you could work for a conservation charity, wildlife organization, or a government. Public relations officers must be aware of all the latest news related to their area of wildlife conservation. They keep in touch with scientists and other conservation workers to learn all they need to know to run campaigns that make people aware of wildlife issues. A degree in marketing is useful.

PUBLIC EDUCATION AND OUTREACH SPECIALIST

You may be interested in a conservation career to help animals, but did you know that a good way to do this is by helping people? Public education and outreach specialists meet with people who live in or near a threatened species or habitat. They teach them about the threats and how this affects local people, too. They help local people learn how to protect and benefit from local wildlife and habitats. A degree in environmental studies is useful in this role.

▲ Public education and outreach specialists explain information in a clear and engaging way.

ENVIRONMENTAL SCIENTIST

Environmental scientists study the effects of human activities on the environment. In this role you would conduct tests and analyze data in order to prevent and solve environmental problems. You would gather samples in the field and conduct tests in the lab. For example, you might collect samples of water and soil from a habitat, then test it for **pollution** caused by industry and farming. You would then study how that pollution might affect habitats and wildlife in the area. A degree in physics or environmental science is usually needed for this career.

GLOSSARY

atmosphere the blanket of gases that surround Earth

breed to produce offspring

captivity kept in an enclosed space, not in the wild

carbon dioxide (CO2) a gas that contributes to climate change when released into the atmosphere

communications the sharing of messages or information

conservation protection of the planet

conservationists people who try and protect the planet

deoxyribonucleic acid (DNA) material that carries all the information about how a living thing will look and function

distinct species a separate species

endangered at risk of becoming extinct, or dying out

environment a natural place where plants and animals live

evidence facts and information that show something exists or is true

fertilizer a substance that helps plants grow

forensics related to the scientific investigation of a crime

fossil fuels fuels formed from the remains of plants and animals that lived long ago

Geographic Information Systems (GIS) computer systems that analyze and display geographical information

geological related to Earth's structure

great apes apes that are large and look similar to humans

habitat a place in which plants and animals live

hydroelectric dam a wall built across a river that allows the water to be used to make electricity

instincts the way animals naturally react or behave

mammals warm-blooded animals that feed their young with milk from their bodies

mate an animal of the opposite sex to breed with

mines human-made openings in the ground made to remove things such as minerals

organisms living things such as plants and animals

overpopulating growing too many in number

parched dried out from heat and lack of water

plantations areas of land on which crops are grown

poaching the illegal killing or capture of animals

policy a plan of action followed by a government, or a group of people

pollution substances that are harmful to living things

population all the people living in a certain area

prehistoric before recorded history

prey animals that are hunted and eaten by other animals

rain forests thick forests of tall trees found in tropical areas that get a lot of rain

reproduction the process by which plants and animals have their young

reserves areas where wildlife can live in safety

resources things that people use

samples small amounts for testing

smuggled taken to or from a place secretly and illegally

species a type of plant or animal

sustainable can be relied upon for the forseeable future

tagged attached an electronic marker to an animal to allow tracking of its movements

termites small, pale soft-bodied insects

territory an area of land that an animal regards as its own and that it may defend from other animals

texture the feel or appearance of the surface of something

timber wood from trees that have been cut down

trade the exchange of goods for money

tropical related to the tropics. Tropics are hot regions found near the equator, an imaginary line around the middle of Earth

FIND OUT MORE

BOOKS

Dickmann, Nancy. *Orangutans* (Fast Track: Animals in Danger). Brown Bear, 2019.

Grack, Rachel. *Orangutans* (Blastoff Readers). Bellwether Media, 2022.

Kington, Emily. *Orangutans* (Animals in Danger). Hungry Tomato, 2022.

WEBSITES

Learn more about orangutans and their forest habitats at:
https://animals.sandiegozoo.org/animals/orangutan

Discover the ultimate guide to careers in conservation at:
www.conservation-careers.com/15-key-conservation-jobs-ultimate-guide-for-conservation-job-seekers

Hear directly from people working in conservation. Find out what they have to say about a career in conservation at:
www.conservation-careers.com/conservation-jobs-careers-advice/how-to-get-a-job-in-conservation

Discover careers in environmental science at:
https://jobs.environmentalscience.org

Find out more about orangutan conservation at:
https://savetheorangutan.org/mission

Find lots of amazing wildlife careers and what they involve at this useful site:
www.thebalancecareers.com/careers-with-wildlife-125918

Discover what the world's leading wildlife organization, the WWF, is doing to help orangutans and how you can get involved:
www.worldwildlife.org/species/orangutan

Publisher's note to educators and parents:
All the websites featured above have been carefully reviewed to ensure that they are suitable for students. However, many websites change often, and we cannot guarantee that a site's future contents will continue to meet our high standards of educational value. Please be advised that students should be closely monitored whenever they access the Internet.

INDEX

apes 4, 5, 8, 38–39

babies 15, 20, 23, 24, 25, 26–27, 34, 35, 39, 40
breeding 16, 20, 29, 36
bushmeat 4, 22

captivity 20, 36–37
careers in conservation 5, 14–15, 19, 25, 31, 36, 37, 41, 42–43, 44–45
classification 7
climate change 28–29, 30, 37, 40, 41
conservation 4, 14–15, 17, 19, 25, 31, 36, 37, 40, 41, 42–43, 44–45
conservationists 4, 5, 14–15, 17, 19, 25, 29, 31, 34, 36, 37, 40, 41, 42–43, 44–45

dams 8, 21
droughts 30, 31

ecosystems 10, 11
extinction 4, 5, 8, 21, 23, 36

farms and farmers 4, 16, 17, 18, 19, 21, 24, 31, 38, 39, 45
females 6, 8, 23, 24, 26, 27, 29, 40
fires 18, 29, 30–31, 37
food and feeding 11, 12–13, 16, 18, 24, 29, 30, 32, 33, 35, 39
forests 4, 5, 6, 7, 8, 9, 10, 11, 15, 16, 17, 18, 19, 21, 23, 24, 25, 29, 30, 31, 33, 34, 35, 37, 38, 39, 40, 41, 43

habitats 4, 5, 6, 7, 8, 9, 10, 11, 14, 15, 16, 17, 18, 19, 20–21, 23, 24, 25, 28, 29, 30, 31, 33, 34, 35, 36, 37, 38, 39, 40, 41, 43, 44, 45
home ranges 8
hunting 4, 21, 22–23, 24, 25, 26, 32, 35, 39

illegal wildlife trade 34, 35, 37, 40
International Union for Conservation of Nature (IUCN) 5

keystone species 10
kids on a mission 5, 15, 17, 23, 29, 35, 41, 43

logging 16, 17, 23, 25, 35

males 6, 7
mates 30
mines and mining 4, 16, 17, 38, 39

night nests 26, 33, 37, 44

other endangered animals 20–21, 38–39

pets 24, 34, 35, 40
plantations 16, 18–19, 23, 24–25, 35
poaching 20, 21, 22, 23, 34, 37, 38, 39, 44

Red List 5
reserves 17, 19, 41, 44

territories 8–9

ABOUT THE AUTHOR

Award-winning author Louise Spilsbury, who also writes under the name Louise Kay Stewart, has written more than 250 books for young people on a wide range of exciting subjects. She especially loves writing about animals and learning more about what we can all do to protect amazing species such as the orangutan.